WITHDRAWN

You Are in Ancient Egypt

Ivan Minnis

Raintree

Chicago, Illinois

© 2005 Raintree
a division of Reed Elsevier Inc.
Chicago, Illinois

Customer Service 888-363-4266

Visit our website at www.raintreelibrary.com

Originated by Dot Gradations Ltd.
Printed in China by South China Printing.

09 08 07 06 05
10 9 8 7 6 5 4 3 2 1

**Library of Congress Cataloging-in-
Publication Data**

Minnis, Ivan.
  You are in ancient Egypt / Ivan Minnis.
    p. cm. -- (You are there!)
  Includes bibliographical references and index.
  Contents: The Egyptian Empire -- The ancient
Egyptians -- Egyptian towns -- Egyptian farms --
Food and drink -- Growing up -- Reading and
writing -- Egyptian art -- Egyptian technology --
Egyptian rulers -- Religious beliefs -- Life after
death.
  ISBN 1-4109-0616-7 (library binding-hardcover) -
- ISBN 1-4109-1008-3 (pbk.)
  1. Egypt--Civilization--To 332 B.C.--Juvenile
literature. [1. Egypt--Civilization--To 332 B.C.] I.
Title. II. You are there (Chicago, Ill.) III. Series.

  DT61 .M553
  932--dc22

2003027742

Acknowledgments
The publishers would like to thank the following
for permission to reproduce photographs:
AKG Images pp. **5** (Erich Lessing), **8** (Erich
Lessing), **11** (Erich Lessing), **12** (Erich Lessing),
17, **18** (Erich Lessing), **19** (Erich Lessing); Alamy
Images (Ian M. Butterfield) p. **22**; Ancient Art
and Architecture pp. **6**, **7** (R. Sheridan), **9**, **10**
(R. Sheridan), **13** (R. Sheridan), **15**, **23**
(R. Sheridan), **24** (J. Stevens), **26** (R. Sheridan),
28 (R. Sheridan); The Ancient Egypt Picture
Library pp. **14**, **29**; Peter Evans pp. **4**, **20**, **27**;
Phil Cooke and Magnet Harlequin pp. **21**, **25**.

Cover photograph of a carved pharaoh head and
obelisk with hieroglyphics in Luxor, Egypt,
reproduced with permission of James Davis Travel
Photography.

Every effort has been made to contact copyright
holders of any material reproduced in this book.
Any omissions will be rectified in subsequent
printings if notice is given to the publishers.

The paper used to print this book comes from
sustainable resources.

Contents

Some words are shown in bold, **like this**. You can find out
what they mean by looking in the Glossary.

A great civilization

About 5,000 years ago, great **civilizations** were beginning to appear all over the world. In southern Europe, the Minoan people were building great palaces. In Asia, cities were being built along the valley of the Indus River, in what is now Pakistan.

The strongest of all these great civilizations was that of the ancient Egyptians. By 2500 B.C.E., the people of Egypt had constructed many great buildings. We can still see some of them today. The kings, or **pharaohs**, of Egypt became rich and powerful.

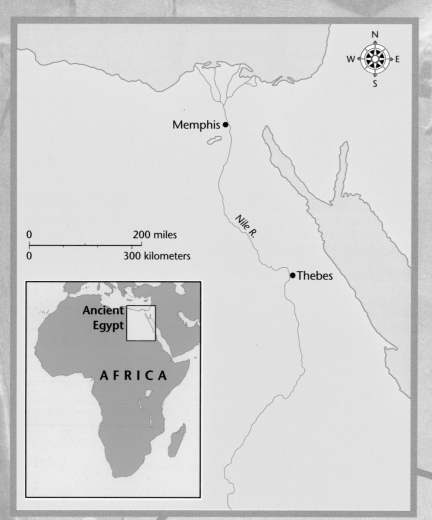

This map shows the location of ancient Egypt. Memphis and Thebes were two of the most important cities.

The Sphinx was a symbol of royal power. It showed a creature that was half lion and half pharaoh.

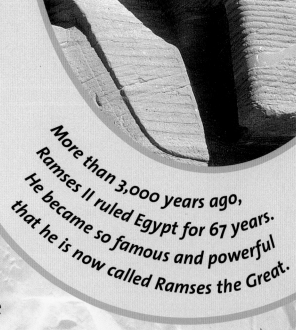

More than 3,000 years ago, Ramses II ruled Egypt for 67 years. He became so famous and powerful that he is now called Ramses the Great.

The greatest pharaoh

Egypt's power lasted for almost 3,000 years. In this book you are going to travel about 3,250 years back in time to Egypt at the time of Ramses II, who ruled from 1279 to 1213 B.C.E. He was one of the greatest of all the pharaohs.

The ancient Egyptians

Imagine walking through an ancient Egyptian town. You can see many different types of people. Rich men and women love fashion and beauty. Poorer people wear clothes that are designed for working hard in the burning sun. You may see some slaves, captured in distant lands by the armies of Ramses II.

Egypt is a very hot country, so people wear light clothes. In this tomb painting, the men are throwing grain in the air to separate the wheat.

Rich and poor

Rich people wear beautiful clothes made of fine **linen**. The women wear valuable jewelry and colorful makeup. Their jewelry is often decorated with colored stones and pictures of the many Egyptian gods. The men wear eye makeup as well.

Poor people dress very simply. Most men wear just a basic linen **loincloth**. This keeps them cool while they work in the hot sun. The women wear simple linen dresses.

Wealthy people wear fine clothes and jewelry.

Finding out about clothes

We know about Egyptian clothes because people have found paintings on Egyptian **tombs** that show what people wore. Clothes and jewelry have also been found in tombs. The Egyptians believed they would need these things in the **afterlife**.

Egyptian towns

Egypt is a desert country. Great cities such as Memphis and Thebes are beside the Nile River. You cannot just turn on a faucet in ancient Egypt. You and your friends have to walk to the river every day to pick up water for cooking and washing. It is much easier to travel to other cities by boat, rather than across the rough desert land.

Every summer the river floods. Then, farmers and their families have to help to move water from the flood on to the fields. This makes the land **fertile** for growing **crops**.

The land along the banks of the Nile River is very fertile.

Your house in ancient Egypt might look something like this model.

Going inside

Your ancient-Egyptian house is probably made of mud bricks and reeds. It has just two or three rooms. Thick walls keep things cool inside. In the evenings, your family will sit on the flat roof. People like to eat and talk there when the sun is not so hot. Rich people's houses are much larger. They may have a garden with a fish pond.

Egyptian farms

When the river floods, it brings water and rich, dark mud to the farmers' fields. After the floods the farmers sow their seeds and wait for the **crops** to grow. The main crops grown are barley and a kind of wheat for bread. Farmers also grow **flax**. This is made into **linen** for their clothes. They grow other crops such as dates, grapes, lettuce, and onions. Animals are important, too. Oxen pull the heavy **plows**. Donkeys carry heavy loads from the fields to the towns.

You might see farmers plowing their fields with the help of oxen.

This **tomb** painting shows a man cutting stalks of grain with a sickle. His wife is behind him with a basket of seed.

Helping with the harvest

Harvest is one of the busiest times of the year. Children like you have to help out. A sharp tool called a sickle is used to harvest the grain. The grain is loaded on to donkeys and taken to be milled into flour. At the mill you can see **scribes** carefully weighing the grain and recording the amount brought by each farmer. Farmers must all give a share of their crop to the **pharaoh** as a **tax**.

Food and drink

There are no refrigerators in ancient Egypt. People have to make fresh food every day. They can bring things they have grown themselves to the market to swap, or barter, for other goods.

You eat freshly baked bread nearly every day. It tastes gritty because the flour is ground on a stone mill. Along with your bread, you may have some vegetables or fruit such as figs or melon. People also eat fish caught in the Nile. Your meal will be washed down with a drink that is made from barley. This drink is so lumpy that you have to drink it through a wooden strainer.

Bread is a very important part of the ancient-Egyptian diet. This model shows a baker grinding corn into flour.

If you go to a feast, you can eat with your fingers. You will have a knife to cut your food.

Food for the rich

You may be lucky enough to eat with a wealthy family. The rich eat much more meat than the poor. They feast on dishes such as antelope, heron, and pelican, as well as roasted pig or sheep. Honey cakes or raisin bread taste sweet, but they will still be gritty and sandy.

Growing up

You and your friends in ancient Egypt do not have much time for playing. Poor children spend most of their lives working hard in the fields with their families. You will have to join in **harvesting** the **crops**. If you are the son of a tradesperson, such as a jeweler or a carpenter, you will learn your father's trade.

Even rich children have a fairly tough life. The boys are sent to school. They start school at the age of five and can leave to get work by the age of twelve.

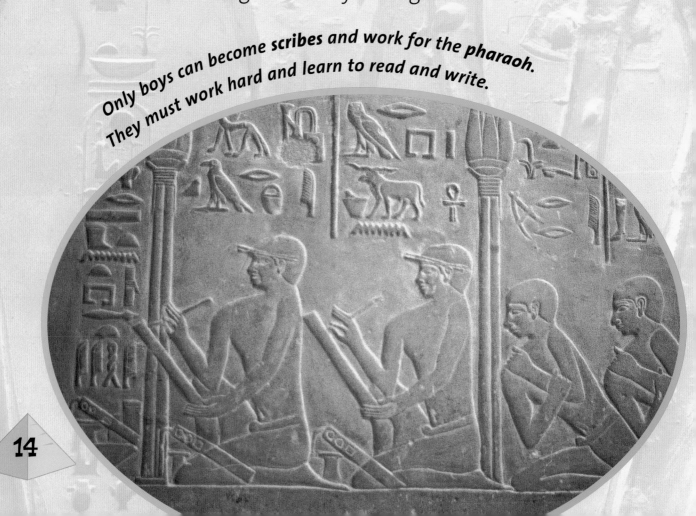

Only boys can become scribes and work for the pharaoh. They must work hard and learn to read and write.

Very few girls go to school. They stay at home and learn how to manage the house. Girls marry about the age of fourteen. Their husbands are usually about sixteen years old.

At play

When there is time, you and your friends play many different games. You can play with balls, dolls, and toy animals such as horses, dogs, and crocodiles.

Finding out about toys

Some toys have been found in the **tombs** of young children. Models of animals were made out of wood and clay. Spinning tops were made from stone, clay, or wood.

If you are lucky enough to have time to play, toys like this wooden horse are popular.

Reading and writing

Boys who go to school can learn to become a **scribe**. Scribes are the smartest men in Egypt. They get the best jobs with the **pharaoh**. They can read and write. Ancient Egyptians write using **hieroglyphics**. The writing is made up of many symbols, or pictures, for different sounds or objects. As a young scribe, you will need to learn and remember more than 700 symbols.

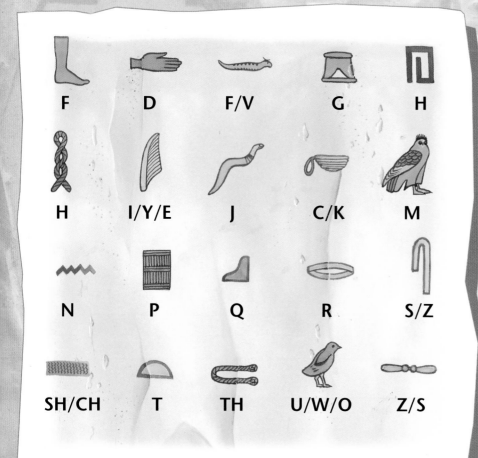

F	D	F/V	G	H
H	I/Y/E	J	C/K	M
N	P	Q	R	S/Z
SH/CH	T	TH	U/W/O	Z/S

Here are some of the symbols you might learn in ancient Egypt.

Finding out about hieroglyphics

For thousands of years, people did not know how to read hieroglyphics. Then, in 1799, the Rosetta Stone was found. It had writing in hieroglyphics as well as in Greek. Because people could read Greek, they could translate the hieroglyphs. They could then read other Egyptian writing in carvings, on papyrus, and on wall paintings.

Many pieces of papyrus have beautiful pictures and hieroglyphs on them.

Paper and ink

The scribes write on a kind of paper called **papyrus**. It is made from the reeds that grow along the banks of the Nile. Reeds are also used as pens, with ink made from charcoal or soot.

Egyptian art

As you travel around ancient Egypt, you will see art everywhere. You do not need to visit an art gallery. Art is painted on the walls of temples, palaces, and public buildings. Some of the best art is hidden away inside the **tombs** of the great **pharaohs**. No one can see this art once the tomb is sealed up. It will help the pharaoh in the **afterlife**.

Once the tomb is sealed, no one can see the paintings.

Egyptian artists always draw people in the same way. Their heads are seen from the side and their bodies from the front and side. Brushes are made from reeds. Plants and **minerals** mixed with water make paints in many beautiful colors. Everyone **respects** artists because they are so skillful. Their art is very important to ancient-Egyptian religion.

Finding out about sculptures

The ancient Egyptians carved many stone statues and figures. Some are huge, like the statues of Ramses II built near the Nile.

There are no cameras in ancient Egypt. Important people are remembered by paintings or statues of themselves.

Egyptian technology

Most people live in one- or two-story houses. The palaces, temples, and statues of Egypt tower above these houses. The ancient Egyptians have no machines or cranes. How do they build these huge **monuments**?

Hundreds of people work together to make these great buildings. They work for the **pharaoh** on his great building projects. Craftspeople use simple tools like hammers, chisels, and saws to cut stone blocks. These blocks are then dragged by the workers to slowly create huge buildings. It is very hard work, especially in the hot sun.

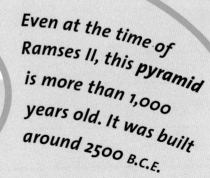

Even at the time of Ramses II, this pyramid is more than 1,000 years old. It was built around 2500 B.C.E.

People use a shaduf, a long pole used to raise or lower a bucket into a well, to take water from the Nile.

Inventions

The ancient Egyptians are great **inventors**. They are one of the first **civilizations** to use the wheel. Soldiers and **officials** use **chariots** with wheels. However, the desert land is harsh and nearly all the villages are along the river. Most travel and **trade** is done by boat along the Nile River.

Pharaohs and law

Egypt is ruled by a **pharaoh**. As well as being king, the people think he is a god. He has complete power over his people and owns most of the land in Egypt. The pharaoh has many palaces around the country.

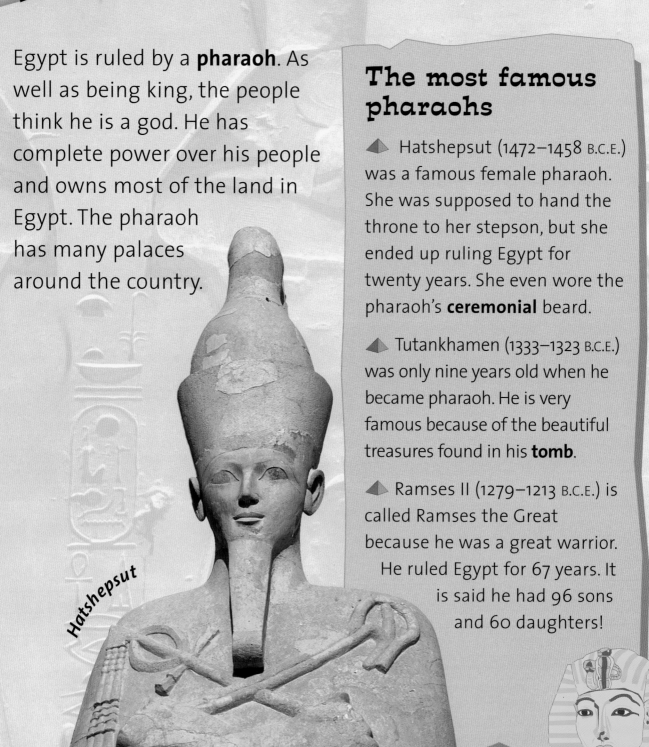

Hatshepsut

The most famous pharaohs

Hatshepsut (1472–1458 B.C.E.) was a famous female pharaoh. She was supposed to hand the throne to her stepson, but she ended up ruling Egypt for twenty years. She even wore the pharaoh's **ceremonial** beard.

Tutankhamen (1333–1323 B.C.E.) was only nine years old when he became pharaoh. He is very famous because of the beautiful treasures found in his **tomb**.

Ramses II (1279–1213 B.C.E.) is called Ramses the Great because he was a great warrior. He ruled Egypt for 67 years. It is said he had 96 sons and 60 daughters!

*The pharaoh's **scribes** write down everything that is **harvested**.*
This makes it easier to collect taxes.

Very few ordinary people ever see the pharaoh. You will
have to follow the orders of the local nobles who
control your village. They have to report to **officials** who
work for the pharaoh. These people collect the **taxes**
and supervise the great building projects. This allows
the pharaoh to make sure his orders are followed.

Religious beliefs

Everyone in ancient Egypt shares the same religious beliefs. They believe that the world is ruled by many different gods. Each god has its own temples. The temples are cared for by priests, who give **offerings** to keep the gods happy. Ordinary people are not allowed inside. Your house has a **shrine** in it. This is so your family can make offerings to the gods who will protect them.

Everyone goes to the temple to celebrate festivals. Only the priests can go inside.

Gods and Goddesses

🔺 Amen-Ra was the king of the gods. He was the main god of the city of Thebes. People believed he protected Egypt from its enemies.

🔺 Osiris was the god of the dead. He was also the god of the **underworld**.

🔺 Isis was the wife of Osiris and was worshiped as the mother goddess.

Ra, god of the Sun.

Osiris

The gods and goddesses have temples all over Egypt. People pray to them for help with all sorts of everyday things.

Life after death

The ancient Egyptians make great preparations for funerals. Rich people have **tombs** built for their families. The tombs are beautifully painted with pictures of gods and goddesses and scenes of daily life.

After death, the body has its insides removed. Then the body is covered with a saltlike powder called **natron**. After 70 days, the body has dried out and is wrapped in bandages. This is called mummification. Once the mummy is wrapped, it can last for thousands of years. The ancient Egyptians believe that the dead person will need their body in the **afterlife**.

Mummies are often buried in beautiful cases.

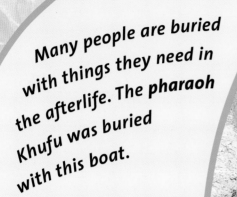

Many people are buried with things they need in the afterlife. The *pharaoh* Khufu was buried with this boat.

Funeral processions

The body is carried to its tomb in a great **procession**. Relatives and friends follow behind. Sometimes people are paid to come to the funeral. They wail and scream to tell everyone that an important person has died. Servants bring gifts to the tomb. These are sealed inside the tomb along with the coffin. The gifts are meant to help the dead person in the afterlife.

Facts for Ancient Egypt

Now you know a bit about ancient Egypt and its people. Here are a few things you need to know to get by in ancient Egypt:

Time

🔺 There are 365 days in the ancient-Egyptian calendar. A new year begins around the time of the Nile flood every year.

🔺 Each week lasts for ten days. Builders work for ten days at a time, with one day off.

Crops can be bartered, or swapped, for goods the farmers cannot make themselves.

Money

There is no money in ancient Egypt. Workers are often paid in wheat or barley. To buy things they do not have, ancient Egyptians have to barter, or swap, them for other things.

Dates to remember:

🔺 About 3000 B.C.E. Egypt is united under King Menes.

🔺 About 2600 B.C.E. the Great **Pyramid** built at Giza.

🔺 In 1323 B.C.E. the boy-king Tutankhamen is buried in the Valley of the Kings.

🔺 In 30 B.C.E. Egypt becomes part of the Roman Empire.

Scales are used by shopkeepers to weigh their goods.

Numbers

Here are the symbols used for ancient Egyptian numbers:

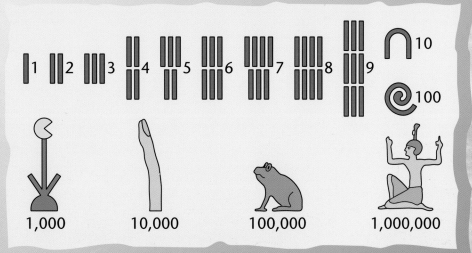

Find out for yourself

You cannot travel back in time to ancient Egypt, but you can still find out lots about the ancient Egyptians and how they lived. You will find the answers to some of your questions in this book. You can also use other books and the Internet.

Books to read

Bailey, Linda. *Adventures in Ancient Egypt*. Minneapolis: Sagebrush Education Resources, 2000.

Balkwill, Richard. *Clothes and Crafts in Ancient Egypt*. Milwaukee, Wis.: Gareth Stevens, 2000.

Kaplan, Leslie. *Home Life in Ancient Egypt*. New York City: Rosen Publishing Group, 2004.

Kaplan, Leslie. *Technology of Ancient Egypt*. New York City: Rosen Publishing Group, 2004.

Nardo, Don. *Ancient Egypt*. Farmington Hills, Mich.: Gale Group, 2002.

Using the Internet

Explore the Internet to find out more about ancient Egypt. Websites can change, so use a search engine such as www.yahooligans.com or www.google.com and type in keywords such as "Tutankhamen," "mummy," "**pyramids**," or "ancient Egypt."

Glossary

afterlife   life that begins after death. The ancient Egyptians believed this was like real life, but perfect.

ceremonial   used for ceremonies, which are acts performed in some regular way according to a set of rules

chariot   two-wheeled vehicle pulled by horses

civilization   united group of people living together

crop   plant grown in large amounts, usually for food

fertile   good for growing crops

flax   crop grown for making linen cloth

harvest   gathering together of the crops for the year

hieroglyphics   pictures and symbols used instead of letters to represent words

invent   make or discover something for the first time

linen   cloth made from flax

loincloth   piece of clothing worn around the hips

mineral   natural, solid substance

monument   structure built to remind people of an event or special person

natron   mineral used for preserving bodies

offering   gift to the gods of animals or other goods

official   important person who works for the pharaoh

papyrus   paperlike material made from papyrus reeds

pharaoh   ruler of the ancient Egyptians

plow   large farming tool, often pulled by animals. Plows churn up the soil and get it ready for planting crops.

procession   group of people moving forward together, often as part of a special ceremony

pyramid   huge tomb made from stone with a square base and triangular sides that join at one point

respect   to honor or look up to another person

scribe   person who could read and write and was employed to do so

shrine   special place which is thought to be holy

tax   forced payment to the government for running a country

tomb   place where someone is buried

trade   buying and selling of things

underworld   place where, according to the ancient Egyptians, a person's spirit goes after death

Index